An Empty, Abandoned House

poems

Joseph Hart

ISBN: 978-81-8253-804-7

First Edition: 2021
Rs. 200/-

Cyberwit.net
HIG 45 Kaushambi Kunj, Kalindipuram
Allahabad - 211011 (U.P.) India
http://www.cyberwit.net
Tel: +(91) 9415091004
E-mail: info@cyberwit.net

Printed at Repro India Limited.

for Gail Belden, we were happy

Wilde was happy.

The bigots got him.

Fanatics have their dreams wherewith the weave
A paradise for a sect; the savage too
From forth the loftiest fashion of his sleep
Guesses at heaven.

- Keats

For the pagan there is no hell.

- Rimbaud

There's enough sorrow on a single street in London
to disprove a thousand loving Gods.

- Wilde

If someone could read every book that has ever been written, all he
could say when he was done
is he'd read a lot of books.

- Sartre

The paradoxes of today are the prejudices of tomorrow.

- Proust

Contents

Love

Stale beer and cheap motel rooms -
Winds that whistle silently
Through old ruins -

Breathless ghosts of people, thoughts
And feelings – love
That never was – is it
All illusion,
Guesses, hope
And fantasy?

Passing music that in time
Will be as common, unremembered
As the prehistoric night -

Lines

The composer who alone -
His genius was his bliss -
Wrote songs that won’t be heard;
God permitted this.

For Edna Millay

Talent isn't learned.
It's just the way you are.
From the brow of Gods
It springs full-grown.
All the brains in Christendom
Do not make a poet.
A light is born in some,
The way is shown.

Lines

Thinking about verse
And how to do it well -
Keats is in a tomb,
As much a poet as a saint.
Have I any value?
Who's to tell?
Let me be like Renoir
Who thought he couldn't paint.

Lines

Some people have a lover
With the happiness it brings.
Years ago the artists
Made poetry that sings.
Americans would scorn
To change their state with kings.
Mine's a sweet content
And happiness with things.

Music

Music makes you fall in love.
Music makes you go to war.
Music makes you feel there is
A God and you're divine.
Music helps you drink your beer.
Music lowers your defenses.
Music makes you burst with tears
Of camaraderie.

Thought in Childhood

Life is like an onion.
You peel away a layer
And there's another layer.
And when you peel them all away,
There's nothing there at all.

My Cat & Burns

The depth of grief and sadness,
Understanding in your eyes.
Despite the thought of Burns, Cat,
What do you know of death?

You sat. I stood there stroking
Your forehead down your back,
And saw such lonely wisdom
As you stared up at me,
Sadness and such wisdom
As you looked up at me.

Talent

To be a famous poet,
As anybody might,
Hope that you have talent
And just write.

Possibly like Gershwin,
It may not happen soon,
You'll write a dozen melodies
To get a pretty tune.

The candle smoke is rising

The candle smoke is rising
Through an infinite geometry,
And I am slowly yielding
To the guardian of sleep, -
The soft caretaker, sleep.

Fragment

If all throughout my soul I feel
A sweet immortal tenderness -
And if my senses apprehend
The soft approach of earth-bound sleep -

Freddy's Love

(a cat)

There was such a love
And happiness in Fred -
Just to be at home,
To love the hand that fed

His pink and tiny mouth.
Fred simply didn't know
In all his little world
Any way to show

His tiny heart's affection.
Who could understand?
So little Fred in love
Sprayed the person's hand.

The person was enraged
And with an angry shout
Picked up little Fred
And put him out.

For Dory Previn

The rhesus monkey and the cloth mother -
The boy and his teddy bear -
The paper describing Jesus
Tossed into the garbage by mistake
So there is no Jesus anywhere or ever -
Is heaven true
Or do I just want it to be?

Grandma

Living in a jungle or a swamp -
Looking at the mirror of a bog -
Listening to angels – and I ask,
"Why is it important to be loved?"

They brutalized my grandma til she died.
Now she's dead and all the pain is gone.
Those who could remember are forgotten.
No one is unhappy in a grave.

Cats

Do cats like wicked people?
They sleep beside the old
And were once entombed with kings
In pyramids of gold.

Maxx

When the little kitten
Sticks his nose into my nostril,
Bites my ear
Or sleeps against my chest -
I think there is a God
Or maybe love
Or maybe something.
But what's the use?
We're aging anyway.

Modern Art

Look at Bernini and hide your face.
Hear Wilde and cease to talk.
Read Keats and Millay and keep your place.
And blush when you hear Bach.

Lines

When there's sweet intelligence
In what the poet wrote,
To read it, like a swell or wave,
Briefly lifts my boat.

Masks

He saw the persona
But not the truth.
He aged in a cloud
From a puzzled youth.

Had he a soul,
He didn't show it.
When he was loved,
He didn't know it.

And when he died,
As everyone does,
He went to a God
That never was.

Heaven

A heaven for martyrs, a heaven for saints -
Saints who do nothing but
Think about God -
A heaven for Black men who
Die with compassion,
Shot by supremacists -
Heaven for gays -
Heaven for people
Without any country -
Heaven for orphans,
Intelligence, cats -

The Angels

Down came criticisms on him,
Constantly and hard,
An incessant hail of pebbles,
Buckshot out of heaven.

He disappeared and withered as
The hateful years continued,
And finally stopped trying to
Avoid another blow.

But in his head was God.
Would even Jesus be a critic?
And heaven. And the angels.
And the sky was filled with light.

One night he went out walking
By a river near the ocean.
God was his salvation.
He was perfect in God's sight.

He was by the sea
Abruptly interrupted,
And overcome by thieves
Who with a gun

And with a club,
Stopped him with the surest
Criticism of them all.

And as he lay dying,
All the sky was filled with wonder,
And he was alone,
Though there were angels in the clouds.

His eyes shut slow at last.
Then with a single pulse he shuddered.
He died.
And all the angels disappeared.

A Story
(for Maxx)

He lived alone with Bach and his cats,
Cziffra and Mozart and Keats,
Sweetly happy. And then one day -
(What causes the ones one meets?) -

He met someone and fell in love.
They lived together a year,
Until his lover went away -
Then nothing but anguish and fear.

With everything gone, he sat alone
And stared at the half-shut door;
And he at last felt lonely,
Who had never felt lonely before.

Gone

A gaunt, drooling, unshaven old man,
Frightened of release,
Is looking at Caravaggio,
And laughing at Matisse.

Will talent ever come again?
Does anybody know?
What is nonsense like Chagall
To Michelangelo?

Lines

He'll tell you it is meaningful.
He'll tell you it is new.
And better than an atavistic ditty.
But what a modern poet
Can never say to you
Is that it is poetical or pretty.

Science

Science is experiment,
Reason, observation.
Who the hell can be opposed to this?
Poke out both your eyes.
Work up a sensation.
And never think.
Religion gives you bliss.

"God's World"
(after Edna Millay)

O world, I cannot hold thee close enough!
    Thy roaches and thy prickly pears!
    Thy rattle snakes, thy grizzly bears!
Thy mustard gas, thine homophobes!
Thine AIDS, thy germs, thy rap, the robes
Around thy white supremacists!
World, world! J. Edgar Hoover's lists!

Long have I known the horrors that appall,
    But never knew I this:
    The deadly nightshade's kiss,
Which sounds like something out of Johnny Keats
Whom critics mock, tuberculosis eats;
My soul – well, I don't have a soul – the Fall
Comes just before the winter. That is all.

Inspiration

I'm God's amanuensis.
I did not write these songs.
I merely took them down.
To someone else belongs

The praise if they are good,
The censure if they're bad.
Even Keats must thank some God
For the genius that he had.

Keats

A single poet, a God!
Is art the only light?
Around him many millions
Who dream, but cannot write.

None of them makes music.
They can't; or think it's smart
Not to. Are the Muses
Dead? And what is art?

Cat Instincts

All the little impulses
That motivate a cat -
Which room to leave or enter -
To sleep in boxes or a hat -
Skinner, Christ or Darwin,
Kindly answer that.

Peace
(my cat)

Maxx slept in my lap
For over half an hour.
While he did, a mood came over me.
I didn't know in nature
There was such a power
That heals –
But music or good poetry.

The Prophet

She thought she was a prophet
And very very wise.
Every day she prayed
To something in the sky.

Then when she turned 70
She had to realize
That Jesus didn't answer
And even prophets die.

Lines

Mystics, saints and madmen
Awaiting a reply
See more than stars and music
In the sky.

Traveling and traveling,
Not going very far -
All the stones in Christendom
Do not make a star.

A Cat's Tail

Tread upon a cat's tail.
He will yelp and run away,
Then cower and look sad as if
He thinks he isn't loved.

Pet him for a moment. He will
Jump into your arms,
Seeming to be happy to
Believe he's loved again.

Two Cats

Devils below -
Angels above -
Freddy is loving -
Maxx is in love -

Lines

Animals love.
It's as simple as that.
I never knew
A bigoted cat.

They don't shoot guns.
They are not cursed
With Gods. Or yell,
"My country first!"

Do cats go to heaven
Or only die?
If they don't go to heaven,
Neither will I.

Love without God -
A wish and a star -
God without love -
That's how things are -

E.L.

When I was young, he said to me,
"Read, read philosophy."
Then let the other slipper fall:
"When you're done, forget it all."

A mind like his – above the herd,
To whom the world must seem absurd.
Yesterday I saw him: old,
A mindless, smiling ember – cold.

Liszt

Like every other poet -
Quick to overrate
His poems, I believe
My poetry is great.

As Liszt when he lay dying
And his pupil mourned the fate
Of his music – then neglected -
Answered, “I can wait.”

Prosody

Once when I was young -
I was once, was I not? -
Poetry and lyrics
Were my chosen lot.

What is verse? I wondered.
I thought and thought and thought
About it, and it seemed
It's rhythm, rhyme - and what?

Prosody

What to write then - ugliness?
Baudelaire, Rimbaud -
Or the self-indulgent formlessness
Of poets in the know?
Or just what makes me happy,
What I love? Although
Everything is mortal,
My poems no less so.
The pyramids and Stonehenge
Are faraway less mortal
Than conceits of rhyme,
And will until they go
(Like sunshine on the snow)
Make a mockery of time.

Love

Don't let Vesuvius erupt on us, Maxx,
A cat but not a pet,
More precious to me than anyone
I have ever met,
Except two boys when I was a boy
Whom I shall not forget
Until I die and the world is gone.
It hasn't happened yet.

Love

Love's an ugly thing.
It makes paupers out of men,
And uses up their youth
So they can never love again.

Insidious and cold,
It's a hateful game to play.
And as the killer leaves,
The dying whispers, "Stay!"

Cats

A cat will sit and stare at you -
Stare and stare and stare at you -
Neither smile nor glare at you -
Just stare and stare and stare.

Paradox

Questions without answers
Decaying in old graves -
The universe has edges.
Light is particles and waves.

The waking dream of madness
Comes somehow from your mother.
This life was unexpected;
So why not another?

Cats & Dogs

Dogs want love
But they slobber and drool.
Cats are loving
But nobody's fool.

Somewhere a cat

Somewhere a cat
Rubs its side against a fence.
That's sleep.
Cobwebs across doorless jambs
Are doors.
That's the moon.
Dark purple wine
Splashes down the sides
Of a lead mug.
That's the night.

What is Chartres?

What is Chartres? Is it a cathedral
Or the brief expression of a concept?
An old, abandon building is condemned.
On one crumbling wall I'll draw my face,
The dearest image and the oldest source,
A perfect likeness of mortality.

Values

After the ball is over
And they call out, "Change partners again!"
Do you sashay back to the first one,
And think of what might have been?

Are you old fashioned and dreamy
Believing in Jesus, not luck,
Problems with only one answer,
And happiness more than a fuck?

That middle class love is what matters,
That madness and aging are lies,
Everyone's basically decent,
And only a person cries?

The Doctor

He asked the wise psychologist,
"Do I love my cat?
I react as if I do. But doctor,
I don't feel a thing.
Am I deeply phony?
Am I possibly insane?"
The doctor smiled profoundly and said,
"No. You're just an ass."

A Tragedy

The farmer left his house
With a mallet and a gun.
"I'm going to kill that dog," he thought,
"And it will be fun."

The little boy just watched.
It was an easy kill.
He didn't do a thing.
And God was very still.

The days continued on,
Though nothing lay ahead.
"I let him kill my dog,"
Was all he ever said.

Dining Out

In a quaint expensive restaurant,
With music most serene,
Sat several Martians dining
On very fine cuisine.

While eating appetizers,
A well-dressed Martian said,
"This person I am eating
Is not entirely dead!"
With manners quite impeccable,
He bit off its head.

A little squirt of blood
Trickled down his chin.
He wiped it off politely
(A moment of chagrin).

Lines

I never said a word -
Never said what I was thinking -
The madness and the thoughts -
Or whether they were true.

Now everyone is gone -
Either dead or dying -
Age! And sparing no one:
Time! I am alone.

Lying on the bank,
Looking back I see the water -
My life – it was a pond -
And the surface never ripples -

Everything I said
Needn't have been spoken -
And everything that mattered -
Since youth – remained as quiet
As an undiscovered grave.

I might say it now
If only I remembered -
To strangers! Just a boring
Curiosity.

Two Stanzas

She died at 96
Happy til the last
Years when she was brutalized.
She's gone. And it is past.

Has mercy any hope?
Has beauty any chance?
When Pinnock plays Scarlatti,
Even angels dance.

Rodgers & Millay

With only several notes
And an interval that's old,
Rodgers made a melody
Of diamonds and gold.

Millay had such a genius
She could make a poem sing,
Even when the subject
Was an ordinary thing.

Lines

Nothing in the world is sane
But animals and music,
Or the columns toted up
In a dusty ledger -

And Horowitz whose music makes
A thousand thousand stars
Bursting through a cloudless night,
Illumining the sea -

While Holding Maxx

Animals love,
Bur they die alone,
Every God
To them unknown.

Maxx will curl
In my coat and sleep.
Is this a love
I can keep

Longer than life?
What can I do?
Do cats love God?
Cats are true.

Truth

Must Truth be so elusive
That just the angels know it?
All the brains in Christendom
Do not make a poet.

Truth! But what is Truth?
Science tries to know.
But reality keeps changing
Every century or so.

Maxx

Maxx lay sleeping on my lap.
I looked down and saw
A thing I'd never seen before;
But I recognized it.

This little beast feels love for me,
A feeling in his body.
He purrs when he is petted; often
Comes when he is called.

Naive

A horrible horrible thing!
But it is perfectly clear -
Bigots and thieves and madmen
Are totally sincere,
And each of them loves his mother
And holds his Jesus dear.

Art

Art that took years – and music -
Integrity, talent – and now
A flash of fame – and it's gone -

Keats

I have written poems
While hiding in the night
That no-one but a madman
In love with Keats could write.

Thinking without rules -
They'll hang you if you do -
But writing such a poem,
Every word of it is true.

Keats declared his aim -
Unguarded as a cat -
To make a thing of beauty.
He did exactly that.

Truth is inspiration -
If there's talent in the beast -
Not beautiful like Keats -
Perhaps poetical, at least -

David

"Now at last I'm strong,"
Little David said;
"And what I was thinking
Is clear inside my head."
Then he went to tell them.
But age got there instead.
When he arrived he found
That all of them were dead.

Lines

God exists only in thought.
While down in the cellar
And up in the attic
And out in the courtyard
Are spectres at play.

Love

Sitting with my cat
Sleeping in my arms
Thinking of a friend -
Did I love any?
Looking at the cat
Trusting unawares -
Why is it important
To be loved?

For Robin

A soft little doggy
All fluffy and white
Sat by a river
And all through the night
He barked at the shadows,
He barked at the stars,
He barked at the water,
He barked at the cars.
He barked and he barked.
Why, this loud little pup
Even barked at the people
His barking woke up!

Bugs

(as you have done to the least of these...)

An American stands tall
Amid violence and hugs.
God made him superior
To animals and bugs.

He puts a tag of death
In a trusting heifer's ear,
Then watches television
With a can of beer.

Love

All the gentle people
Desperate for love -
To me it never mattered.
Why is that?
I can see the feeling -
Gentle and benign -
But not in people -
Only in my cat.

Back From Oz

"The Wizard of Oz" is a lot of fun,
But I must appeal
To sense. Perhaps she dreamed the witch,
But old Miss Gulch is real,
And she'll be back for the dog when Dorothy's
Head begins to heal.

Finish

Cast away love,
Science and God -
At 96 years
None of them matters -
And all that was good
Like music and art
Decays in a brain,
Becoming forgotten -

Cats

When I think about cats
I forget about God,
Sweet little beasts
With the tiniest instincts,
The smallest of loves,
Born just to perish
Like everything else.
Heavenly God,
What's the purpose of that?

Lines

Several years on the planet to wonder -
To listen to music,
To look at a statue -
They think they're precocious and gloat,
"I wrote poems in my youth."
Sarah Chang who has talent
Played the violin at 7.
Illusion – not Christ -
Is the Savior.
Conceit keeps artists young.

J.T.

Sitting in a chair I was
Weeping and hysterical.
With a shoe I hit my head. And he
Crying stuck out both his arms
And ran to me. I put
My hand against his face and shoved him
Back across the room.

J.T.

There he sleeps, his arms outspread,
Across a rumpled morning bed.
And to my eyes he seems to be
Just on the verge of memory,
With nothing unsaid.

Unseeing, although seen by me,
He sleeps in greater liberty.
And every dream inside his head
Is a book I never read,
An unheard melody.

How can this Prince of Consciousness
So beautifully dress
His countenance with tenderness
And consequently bless
His perfect nakedness
With such exquisite harmony
Upon a rumbled bed?

1972

Gertrude Stein

I read a book by Gertrude Stein.
I liked it. And it stirred
An urge to read another.
I bought one. Am I dense?
I read some and I didn't
Understand a word.
Only life, not art,
Should not make sense.

John & Mary

John and Mary – both of them are gone,
Long ago. Though time continues on,
And like an ocean wave across the shore,
Erases – quoth the Raven, "Nevermore" -

I cannot keep the thought of them at bay -
Or like a wizard, wave them both away.
With the soft forgetting of the sea,
I'm waiting for the hour I can say,
"The sting is gone. It's just a memory."

Lines

I loved him forever.
He loved me a day.
Fetch up a casket
To take me away,
A heartless cadaver,
A corpse with no soul.
And off through the rain
Let the little cart roll
That carries my body
With nothing inside,
Gone like a wave
That goes out with the tide,
Over the cobblestones
Roughly I'll ride.
And no one will know
Or remember I died.
There on the bed
Of a small wooden cart,
Take my cadaver
That hasn't a heart,
Plod an old horse
Through the miserable rain,
Down to the graveyard
Where nothing feels pain.
I perished for love,
And I perished in vain,
Bones and a body,
And organs and brain,

But never a heart.
No, never again!
Deep, deep in a hole
Shall my body remain
Til worms have devoured it.
I am insane.

I have a BA. I've had poems published in small magazines and was twice nominated for a Pushcart. A chapbook I wrote entitled "Poems Published in India" was accepted by Kelsay Books. And two collections of poems ("For Kitty" and "Idle Fancies") were published by Cyberwit.net. My favorite poet is Keats.

www.ingramcontent.com/pod-product-compliance
Lightning Source LLC
Chambersburg PA
CBHW050023170726
48282CB00025B/523
* 9 7 8 8 1 8 2 5 3 8 0 4 7 *